Nick Beare

English World

Grammar Practice Book

3

Macmillan

A note to teachers, parents and children

Welcome to the *English World* Level 3 Grammar Practice Book. In this book you will find a variety of activities which practise the grammar points in Pupil's Book 3 and Workbook 3. There are also activities which practise writing skills and phonics/spelling.
These activities can be used in class or for homework.

There is a unit in the Grammar Practice Book for each unit in the Pupil's Book and the Workbook. There are three pages in each unit:
- **Page 1 of each unit** practises the **main grammar point** of the unit.
- **Page 2 of each unit** practises the **Grammar in Conversation** point.
- **Page 3 of each unit** has a **Grammar Castle** activity, which practises the grammar points from pages 1 and 2; and a *Use of English* activity which practises the content of the Workbook *Use of English* page.

The **Review pages** practise the grammar and the phonics and spelling from the previous three units.

Each grammar activity in the Review units has a score out of 5. The phonics and spelling activity has a score out of 10. This gives a total score of 35. The children write their score for the Review pages in a box on the page. They can assess their level of achievement by reading the comments in the **Score Box**.

When all the activities in each unit are complete, the Grammar Practice Book will be a useful reference and revision aid for the children. The series of Grammar Practice Books builds up into a complete record of the grammar in *English World*.

The children can keep their Grammar Practice Books and use them for reference in later levels of *English World*. In this way, they develop good study skills and make an important step to becoming independent learners.

Contents

	page
Unit 1	4
Unit 2	7
Unit 3	10
Review 1	13
Unit 4	17
Unit 5	20
Unit 6	23
Review 2	26
Unit 7	30
Unit 8	33
Unit 9	36
Review 3	39
Unit 10	43
Unit 11	46
Unit 12	49
Review 4	52

Unit 1

It was sunny yesterday.
The children were not in park.
Was the teacher in the classroom? Yes, she was.
Was the teacher in the park? No, she wasn't.

Yesterday

1 Write *was*, *was not*, *were* or *were not*.

1 The boy ____was____ happy.
2 It _____ sunny.
3 The children _____ sad.
4 The children _____ at the zoo.
5 _____ it cloudy? Yes, it _____
6 _____ the children happy? Yes, they _____
7 _____ the children sad? No, they weren't.
8 _____ it cold? No, it wasn't.

2 Write in the correct order. Complete the answers.

1 it / sunny / was ?
___Was it sunny?___ ___No___, ___it___ wasn't.

2 sad / the / was / boy / ?
_____ _____, _____ wasn't.

3 zoo / was / the / fun / ?
_____ Yes, it _____

4 interesting / the / animals / were / ?
_____ Yes, they _____

5 children / the / at / school / were / ?
_____ _____, _____ weren't.

What is the time?
It is quarter past two.

It is quarter to three.

1 Match the times with the clocks.

1 It is quarter past five. _____
2 It is five o'clock. _____
3 It is quarter to five. _____
4 It is quarter to twelve. _____
5 It is quarter past eleven. _____
6 It is seven o'clock. _____

2 Write the times.

1 _____

2 _____

3 _____

3 Write the conversation.

_____

_____ time?

Unit 1 Grammar in conversation

1 Write. Use the words in the circles.

Grammar Castle

Yesterday at the castle

1 He — in the car.   He was in the car.

2 He — in the garden. _____

3 They — in the garden. _____

4 she — in the castle — ? _____

Use of English

2 Circle the nouns in the box. Write them in the sentences.

| book | elephant | piano | big | buy |
| pencil | sandwiches | shells | write | happy |

1 My sister can play the _____.
2 There's an _____ in the zoo.
3 I like _____ for lunch.
4 He's reading a _____.
5 She's drawing with a _____.
6 There are _____ on the beach.

Unit 1 Nouns

Unit 2

He walked to school.
He did not walk to the park.

1 Choose and write.

talked   did not talk

1 She __did not talk__ to her friend.
2 She _____ to her mother.

watched   did not watch

3 She _____ the birds.
4 She _____ the dog.

help   did not help

5 She _____ her father.
6 She _____ her brother.

2 Write about the boy.

talk

1 his friend   __He talked to his friend.__
2 his sister   __He did not talk to his sister.__

climb

3 the tree   _____
4 the gate   _____

walk

5 to school   _____
6 to the park _____

Yesterday

Yesterday

Unit 2   Grammar   7

Did she visit her friend? Yes, she did.
Did she watch television? No, she didn't.

1 Complete the questions and answers.

1 _____ they _____ their grandmother? Yes, they _____
2 _____ he _____ television? No, _____ didn't.
3 _____ he _____ football? Yes, he _____
4 _____ they _____ to the park? Yes, _____ did.
5 _____ she _____ computer games? Yes, she _____

2 Write the words in the correct order. Match with the answers.

1 climb / a tree / did / she / ?   a Yes, he did.
   Did she climb a tree?   c

2 they / did / to the park / go / ?   b No, he didn't.
   _____   ___

3 they / visit / their / friends / did / ?   c Yes, she did.
   _____   ___

4 he / a book / did / read / ?   d No, she didn't.
   _____   ___

5 play / computer games / he / did / ?   e Yes, they did.
   _____   ___

6 a book / did / read / she / ?   f No, they didn't.
   _____   ___

Unit 2 Grammar in conversation

Grammar Castle

1 Write sentences.

Yesterday at the castle

He
play / computer games

1 _He played computer games._

read / a book

2 _He didn't read a book._

They
play / football

3 _____

climb / trees

4 _____

2 Write questions. Complete the answers.

she / a book

1 _Did she read a book_ ?
Yes, she _did._

they / trees

2 _____?
No, _____ didn't.

he / computer games

3 _____?
Yes, he _____.

Use of English

3 Circle the adjectives in the box. Write them in the sentences.

hot	jump	cold
monster	happy
funny	fish	tired
ugly	push

1 I don't like snakes. They're _ugly._

2 I'm wearing shorts. It's a _____ day.

3 I'm wearing a coat. It's a _____ day.

4 It's my birthday. I'm _____!

5 I'm going to bed. I'm _____.

6 I'm laughing. This book is _____.

Unit 2 Adjectives   9

Unit 3

The plane is faster than the car.

1 Compare the animals.

1 soft   The mouse is ___softer___ than the ant.
2 big   The mouse is _____ than the ant.
3 fast   The mouse is _____ than the ant.
4 long   The mouse is _____ than the ant.
5 small   The ant is _____ than the mouse.
6 slow   The ant is _____ than the mouse.

2 Write about the pictures.

long / short

1 ___The train is longer than the car.___
2 ___The car is shorter than the train.___

big / small

3 _____
4 _____

fast / slow

5 _____
6 _____

tall / short

7 _____
8 _____

10 unit 3 Grammar

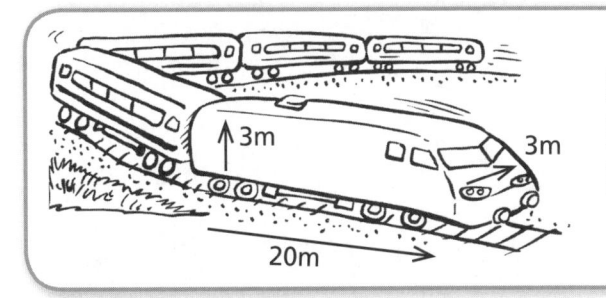

How tall is it? It's 3 metres tall.
How wide is it? It's 3 metres wide.
How long is it? It's 20 metres long.

1 Match and complete with tall, wide or long.

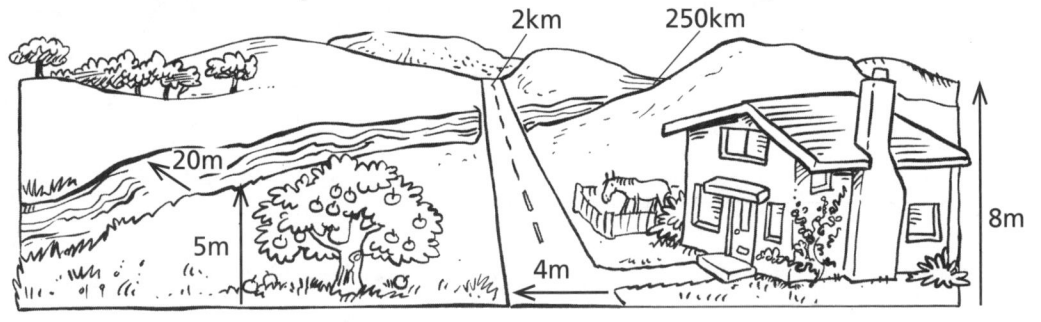

1	How wide is the river?	_e_	a It's 250 kilometres _____
2	How long is the river?	_____	b It's 5 metres _____
3	How tall is the tree?	_____	c It's 8 metres _____
4	How tall is the house?	_____	d It's 2 kilometres _____
5	How wide is the road?	_____	e It's 20 metres _wide._
6	How long is the road?	_____	f It's 4 metres _____

2 Complete. Use the words in the box.

| How long | How tall | How wide | wide | tall | long |

1 _____ is he? He's 1 metre 35 centimetres _____

2 _____ is the garden? It's four metres _____

3 _____ is the path? It's twenty metres _____

Unit 3 Grammar in conversation   11

Grammar Castle

1 Write sentences.

tall   the castle / the tree

1 <u>The castle is taller than the tree.</u>

fast   the car / the bicycle

2 _____

big   the dog / the cat

3 _____

old   the castle / the car

4 _____

2 Write the words in the correct order. Answer the questions.

tall / the / how / tree / is / ?

1 <u>How tall is the tree?</u>   <u>It's 5 metres tall.</u>

tower / is / how / the / tall / ?

2 _____?   _____

the / is / path / how / long ?

3 _____?   _____

Use of English

3 Circle the verbs in the box. Write them in the sentences.

I can <u>climb</u> that tree.

1 Can you _____ this toy for me, please?

2 Please _____ the door.

3 _____ at my new watch!

4 Don't _____ the flowers!

5 Does your friend _____ good pictures?

pick	paint
huge	(climb)
friendly	open
lion	mend
look	bread

12 **Unit 3** Verbs

Review 1 — Review of Unit 1 to Unit 3

> He was / was not at home.
> They were / were not happy.
> Was he at home? Yes, he was. / No, he wasn't.
> Were they happy? Yes, they were. / No, they weren't.

1 Complete with *was*, *were*, *was not* or *were not*.

They were at school. They ___were not___ at home.

1 Jack was at home. He _____ at school.
2 _____ you at school yesterday? Yes, I _____
3 _____ they at school yesterday? Yes, they _____
4 Where _____ he? He was at home.
5 Where _____ they? They were at school.

Score ____ /5

> What is the time? It is quarter to four / four o'clock / quarter past four

2 Write about the time.

It's quarter past four.

4 _____ time?

1 It's _____
   It's _____

2 It's _____
5 What's _____?

3 It's _____
   It's _____

Score ____ /5

Review 1   13

Review 1

> We walked to school. We did not walk to the beach.

3 Write sentences.

(talk) They __talked__ to their friends.
(not walk) They __did not walk__ in the park.
1 (play) They _____ tennis.
2 (not listen) They _____ to music.
3 (help) Jack _____ his mother.
4 (not help) Tom _____ his mother.
5 (watched) Lucy _____ television.

Score ____ /5

> Did they play in the park? Yes, they did. / No, they didn't.

4 Make questions. Write answers with *Yes*.

They walked in the park.
__Did they walk in the park?__ ? __Yes, they did.__

He climbed the tree.
1 _____? _____

The sheep lived in the barn.
2 _____? _____

They watched the cows.
3 _____? _____

Max talked to the sheep.
4 _____? _____

Lily helped her friends.
5 _____? _____

Score ____ /5

Review 1

Review 1

> How tall / long / wide is it?
> It's ten metres tall / long / wide.

5 Write questions and answers.

How long is the car? It's 3 metres _long._

1 _____ is the river? It's 30 metres wide.

2 _____ is the tree? It's 5 metres tall.

3 _____ is the pencil? It's 6 centimetres long.

4 How high is the mountain? It's five hundred metres _____

5 How wide is the road? It's four metres _____

Score ____ /5

Phonics and spelling

6 Write and say.

jar

ar
1 _____
2 _____
3 _____

ou
4 _____
5 _____
6 _____

ay
7 _____
8 _____
9 _____
10 _____

y-s-a-t

Score ____ /10

20–25   26–30   31–35

My score is _____.

Review 1   15

Review 1

Your Writing Page

1 Complete the story about the picture. Use the words in the box.

Jack was at the beach on _____. It was _____.
He walked on the _____. He played _____.
The fish were in the _____. They were _____.

| sea | pretty | sand |
| Monday | hot | football |

2 Write about the picture. Use the words in the box.

| Tuesday | cold | path |
| basketball | birds | trees | noisy |

Emma was in the park on _____
_____
_____
_____

Unit 4

Did they travel in cars? No, they didn't.
Did they travel in wagons? Yes, they did.

1 Write.

need	food	They didn't need food.
	wood	They needed wood.

| travel | in a wagon | 1 _____ |
| | in a car | 2 _____ |

| stop | near a river | 3 _____ |
| | near a beach | 4 _____ |

2 Write questions. Choose the correct answer.

cook / fish

1 <u>Did they cook fish?</u>   Yes, they did.   No, they didn't.

play / with a ball

2 _____?   Yes, they did.   No, they didn't.

fetch / wood

3 _____?   Yes, they did.   No, they didn't.

travel / in a helicopter

4 _____?   Yes, they did.   No, they didn't.

Unit 4   Grammar   17

They did not travel in trains.

1 Find the mistakes in the pictures. Write sentences with the words in the boxes.

| play | wear | eat | live | watch | travel |

| television | big houses | shorts |
| pizzas | cars | computer games |

1 _They did not eat eat pizzas._
2 _____
3 _____
4 _____
5 _____
6 _____

2 Think about life in your town a hundred years ago. Write about what people did not do.

1 use / computers _____
2 eat / burgers _____
3 travel / in planes _____
4 play / basketball _____

18 Unit 4 Grammar in conversation

1 Complete with the correct form of the verbs.

Grammar Castle in 1600

1 play   They _played_ games with a ball.
2 travel   They _____ on horses.
3 not, use   They _____ telephones.
4 not, travel   They _____ in planes.
5 cook ?   _____ they _____ burgers? No, they didn't.
6 watch ?   _____ they _____ television? No, they didn't.

Use of English

2 Write the past forms of the verbs. Add the past forms to the crossword.

Across
1 pull _pulled_
5 chop _____
8 skip _____
9 need _____
10 travel _____

Down
2 fetch _____
3 cook _____
4 stop _____
6 play _____
7 use   _____

Unit 4   Past tense spelling rules

Unit 5

There was a car in the window.
Was there a boat? Yes, there was.
Were there trains? No, there weren't.

1 Write *was*, *was not*, *were* or *were not*.

1 There _____ a boat.
2 There _____ five cars.
3 There _____ a cow.
4 There _____ dogs.
5 _____ there a drum? Yes, there _____
6 _____ there sweets? No, there weren't.

2 Write about the toyshop.

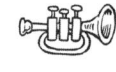

1 __There was a robot.__
2 _____ 
3 _____ 
4 __Were there dolls?__   Yes, there were. 
5 _____?   No, there wasn't. 
6 _____?   No, there weren't. 

20 Unit 5 Grammar

How much is the boat? It is £10.
How much does the train cost? It costs £20.

1 Work out the prices. Complete the questions and answers.

£ wot
£ xsi
£ ifnetfe
£ ifev

1 How _____ is the boat? It's _____
2 _____ much _____ the train _____? _____ costs _____
3 _____ much _____ the drum? It's _____
4 _____ _____ does the guitar _____? It _____ _____

2 Write pairs of questions and answers.

£75   £89   £23   £5

How much is ....   How much does ...

1 How much is the mobile phone?   How much does the mobile phone cost?
   It's £75.   It costs £75.

2 How much is the bike?   _____?
   It's £89.   _____

3 _____?   How much does the computer game cost?
   _____   It costs £23.

4 How much is the ball?   _____?
   It's £5.   _____

Unit 5 Grammar in conversation 21

1 Complete.

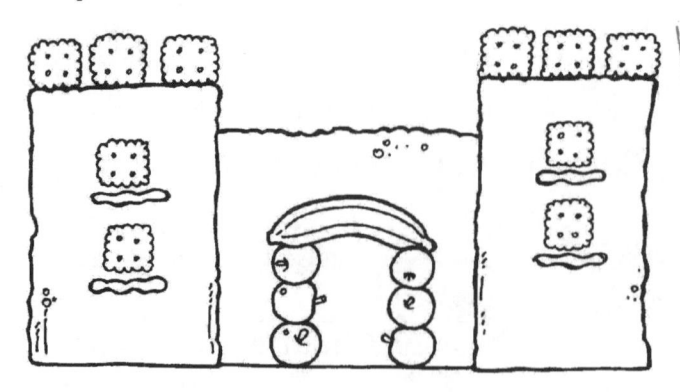

Grammar Castle

Grammar Castle Café
Castle burger £4
Castle sandwich £2
Castle pizza £3

The Grammar Castle cake yesterday

1 There _____ six apples.
2 There were _____ biscuits.
3 _____ there a banana? Yes, there _____.
4 _____ there sandwiches? No, _____ weren't.
5 _____ is the Castle pizza? It's £3.
6 How much _____ the Castle burger cost? It _____ £4.
7 _____ much does the Castle sandwich _____? It costs £2.

Use of English

2 Write the comparative forms of the adjectives. Add the comparative forms to the crossword.

Across
6 angry _____
7 thin _____

Down
1 hot _____
2 large _____
3 fat _____
4 happy _____
5 funny _____

6 angrier

unit 5 Comparative adjectives - spelling rules

Unit 6

They won the prize.
Did they win the prize? Yes, they did.

1 Write about Joe's day

1 go   He __went__ to his friend's house.
2 see   He _____ his new computer.
3 say   He _____ "Let's play a computer game."
4 sit   He _____ next to his friend.
5 win   He _____ the game.
6 say   His friend _____ "You're brilliant!"
7 come   He _____ home.

2 Write sentences using *did not*.

he / win / a football match
1 __He did not win a football match.__

he / sit next to / his sister
2 _____

he / go / the park
3 _____

he / see / his new mobile phone
4 _____

he / win / a prize
5 _____

I like play**ing** basketball.

1 Write about Ryan. Use the verbs in the box.

| read | eat | win |
| listen | play | phone |

1 He likes ___reading___ books.
2 He _____ _____ burgers.
3 _____ _____ _____ to music.
4 Does he _____ _____ prizes? Yes, he does.
5 _____ he _____ _____ computer games? Yes, he does
6 _____ _____ _____ _____ friends? Yes, he does.

2 Complete the sentences and questions. Answer the questions.

1 Do you _____ playing football?

2 _____

3 _____ you like _____ friends?

4 _____

5 _____ eating onions?

6 _____, I don't.

24 Unit 1 Grammar in conversation

1 Write sentences about this boy's day at Grammar Castle.

My day at Grammar Castle

1 win / a prize _____He won a prize._____
2 see / the flags _____
3 not go / the shopping centre _____
4 not win / the race _____

2 Write in the correct order.

1 he / going / like / to the castle / does /
_____? Yes, he does.

2 pictures of the castle / does / like / drawing / he /
_____? No, he doesn't.

Use of English

3 Change the adjectives to adverbs. Write the adverbs in the crossword.

Across
3 quick _quickly_
4 tired _____
7 pretty _____
8 sad _____
9 loud _____

Down
1 bright _____
2 noisy _____
3 quiet _____
5 slow _____
6 easy _____

Unit 6 Adverbs 25

Review 2 — Review of Unit 4 to Unit 6

> They travelled in a train.
> They did not travel in a car.

1 Write sentences.

	travel	They	___travelled___	in a car.
	not, travel	They	___did not travel___	in a bus.
1	see	They	_____	cows.
2	not, see	They	_____	sheep.
3	play	They	_____	tennis.
4	not, play	They	_____	football.
5	not, read	They	_____	books.

Score ___ /5

> Did they play with a ball? Yes, they did. / No, they didn't.

2 Write questions.

___Did they play___ football? No, __they__ didn't.
1 _____ cows? Yes, they _____
2 _____ in a bus? _____, they didn't.
3 _____ sheep? _____, they didn't.
4 _____ in a car? _____, they did.
5 _____ tennis? Yes, they _____

Score ___ /5

26 Review 2

Review 2

There was / was not a car.
There were / were not trains.

3 Write about the picture.

    <u>There were</u> birds.
    <u>There was not</u> a mouse.
1 _____ a frog.
2 _____ cats.
3 _____ flowers.
4 _____ a dog.
5 _____ a fish.

My garden yesterday

Score ____ /5

Was there a car? Yes, there was. No, there wasn't.
Were there trains? Yes, there were. No, there weren't.

4 Write questions about the garden in 3. Match with the answers.

    flowers <u>Were there flowers?</u>   <u>c</u>
1 a fish   _____? ____ a Yes, there was.
2 birds   _____? ____ b No, there wasn't.
3 a frog   _____? ____ c Yes, there were.
4 a dog   _____? ____ d No, there weren't.
5 cats   _____? ____

Score ____ /5

Review 2

Review 2

How much is the sandwich? It's £2.
How much does the sandwich cost? It costs £2.
I like using computers.

4 Write in the correct order.

is / How / the cake / much /

___How much is the cake?___   It's £3.

much / the pizza / does / How / cost /

1 _____? It costs £6.

is / much / the train / How /

2 _____? It's £5.

likes / she / basketball / playing

3 _____

Phonics and spelling

5 Write and say.

1 ow   snow
2 ow   _____
3   _____
4 er   _____
5   _____

6 ir   _____
7   _____
8   _____
9   _____
10   _____

Score ____ /10

20–25   26–30   31–35

My score is _____.

Review 2

Your Writing Page

1 Complete the story about the picture. Use the words in the box.

| going to the zoo | tigers | zoo | Saturday |
| friends | bus | elephant |

On _____ I went to the _____ with my _____. We travelled in a _____. We saw the animals. There were lions and there was an _____. There weren't _____. I like _____!

2 Write about the picture. Use the words in the box.

| Sunday | park | family | car | played games |
| slides | roundabout | swings | going to the park |

On <u>Sunday I went to</u> _____
_____
_____
_____

Review 2

Unit 7

She had a book. She did not have an iPod*.
Did she have a book? Yes, she did.
Did she have an iPod? No, she didn't.

*iPod is a trademark of Apple Inc.

1 Complete with *have*, *had* or *did not have*.

1 She _____ an iPod.

2 He _____ a drink.

3 They _____ bags.

4 They _____ books.

5 Did she _____ a sandwich? No, she did not.

6 Did she _____ a drink? Yes, she did.

2 Correct the mistakes.

He had brown hair. (black hair).

1 <u>He didn't have brown hair.</u>   <u>He had black hair.</u>

She had long hair. (short hair)

2 _____   _____

They had motorbikes. (cars)

3 _____   _____

He had a pizza. (sandwich)

4 _____   _____

30 unit 7 Grammar

You must be quiet.
You must not shout.
Must we be quiet? Yes, you must.

1 Write *must* or *must not*.

1 You _____ get up early.
2 You _____ get up late.
3 You _____ listen to ipods.
4 You _____ clean your room every day.
5 _____ we run for half an hour before breakfast? Yes, you _____

2 Write the girl's conversation with her mother.

1 We must not sing.   sing

get up early   2 Must you get up early?

3 Yes, we must. And _____ go to bed late

clean your room   4 _____?

5 Yes, we _____

What about computer games?

6 We _____. It's terrible!   play computer games

I think it's very good for you!

Unit 7 Grammar in conversation

1 Write about Tom.

Tom was at Grammar Castle yesterday.

1 He _____ an iPod.
2 He _____ have a sandwich.
3 _____ a bag? _____, _____ didn't.
4 _____ he _____ a camera? Yes, he _____

2 Write the rules for the Monster Ride at Grammar Castle. Use the words in the box.

Rules
sit down 1 _You must sit down._   stand up 3 _____
     eat 2 _____   buy a ticket 4 _____

Use of English

3 Write prepositions for the pictures.

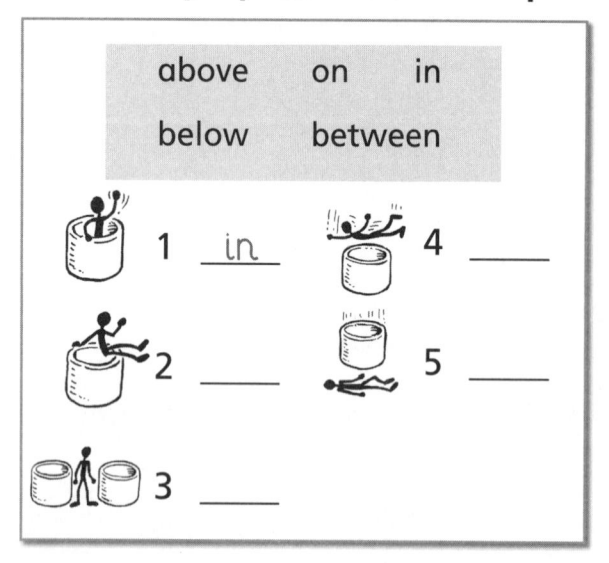

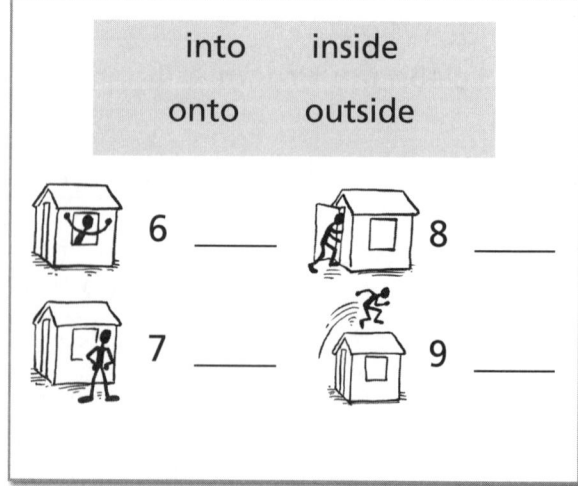

above	on	in
below	between	

1 _in_
2 ____
3 ____
4 ____
5 ____

into	inside
onto	outside

6 ____
7 ____
8 ____
9 ____

unit 7 Prepositions

Unit 8

> She saw the horse.
> She did not see the boat.
> Did she see the boat? No, she didn't.

1 Complete the story with the past forms of the verbs.

1 buy   Amy _____ a dress in a shop.

2 fall   Her purse _____ on the floor.

3 find   Lucy _____ Amy's purse.

4 take   Lucy _____ the purse to the information desk.

5 see   Amy _____ Lucy at the information desk.

2 Write pairs of sentences.

    Amy   buy   a T-shirt
                             a dress

1 <u>Amy did not buy a T-shirt.</u>   <u>She bought a dress.</u>
    Amy   lose   her mobile phone
                            her purse

2 _____ _____
    Lucy   see   Amy's mobile phone
                            Amy's purse

3 _____ _____

Unit 8 Grammar

Where did they go? To the shopping centre
What did they buy? Two jackets
How much did they spend? £20

1 Complete. Use the correct forms of the verbs in the box.

go   spend   buy   eat

They _____ to the theme park.
They _____ £30.
They _____ burgers.
They _____ T-shirts.
_____ they _____ sandwiches? No, they didn't.
_____ they _____ to sports centre? No, they didn't.
_____ they _____ caps? No, they didn't.

2 Write questions. Match with the answers.

When / go?

1 <u>When did they go?</u> <u>b</u>   a Burgers

Where / go?

2 _____? ____   b On Saturday

How much / they spend?

3 _____? ____   c At 7.30

What / buy in the shop?

4 _____? ____   d £30

What / have for lunch?

5 _____? ____   e Infinity Theme Park

What time / come home?

6 _____? ____   f T-shirts

34 Unit 8   Grammar in conversation

Grammar Castle

The Gift Shop at Grammar Castle

I had a great time at Grammar Castle yesterday!

1 Complete the sentences.

go
1 She _____ to Grammar Castle yesterday.
2 She _____ _____ _____ to the park.

lose
3 Did she _____ her mobile phone? No, she didn't.
4 She _____ her purse.

2 Write questions and answers.

What / she / lose?
1 _____? _____

Where / she / lose / her purse?
2 _____? _____

When / she / go / to the shop?
3 _____? _____

Use of English

3 Write the past tense forms of the verbs. Add the past tense forms to the crossword.

Across
3 hurry *hurried*
7 stop _____
8 need _____
9 smile _____
10 carry _____

5 cry _____
6 use _____

Down
1 hop _____
2 like _____
4 travel _____

Unit 8 Past tense spelling rules 35

Unit 9

> Which boy is the tallest?
> Matt is the tallest.

1 Compare the animals.

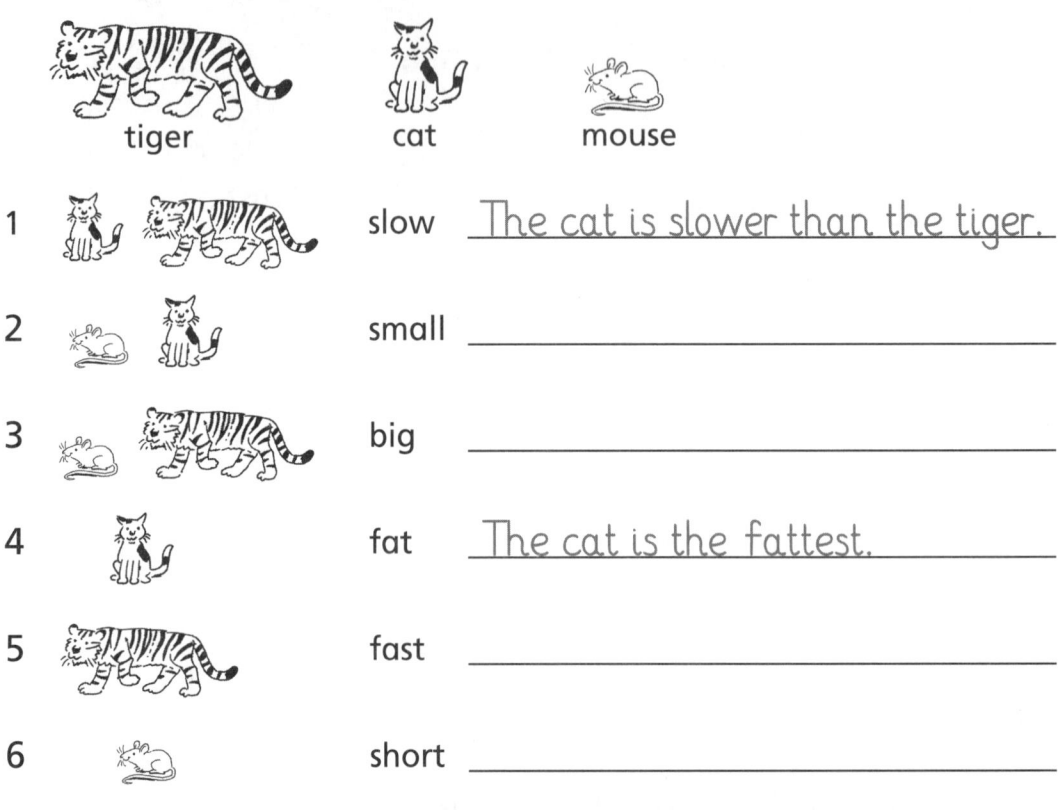

tiger   cat   mouse

1 slow   The cat is slower than the tiger.

2 small   _____

3 big   _____

4 fat   The cat is the fattest.

5 fast   _____

6 short   _____

2 Write questions with the adjectives in the box. Match with the answers.

| fat small big long tall |

1 Which animal is the fattest?   b

2 _____ ? ___

3 _____ ? ___

4 _____ ? ___

5 _____ ? ___

a The tiger
b The cat
c The mouse

Why are you smiling? Because I'm happy.

1 Match.

1 Why is she smiling? ____   a Because she hurt her foot
2 Why is she crying? ____   b Because she is the winner.
3 Why is he sleeping? ____   c Because it's late.
4 Why is she shouting? ____   d Because it's very hot.
5 Why are they drinking? ____   e Because she can see a mouse.

2 Write questions with Why ...? Choose the reasons and write the answers with Because ...

1 <u>Why is she smiling?</u>   <u>Because it is her birthday.</u>
2 _____ ?   _____
3 _____ ?   _____

3 Write the questions and answers in 2 as sentences.

1 <u>She is smiling because it is her birthday.</u>
2 _____
3 _____

Unit 9 Grammar in conversation

1 Compare the horses.

The Horses at Grammar Castle

1 Tiny is _the smallest._
2 Harry is _____.
   fast   slow
3 Flash is _____
4 Harry is_____
   fat   thin
5 Harry is _____ and _____
   young   old
6 Which horse is _____? Harry.
7 _____ horse is _____? Tiny.

Harry   Flash   Tiny

2 Write a question and answer about Harry.
Why _____? _____ hungry.

Use of English

2 Write a pronoun for each word. Add the pronouns to the crossword.

Across

1 the cat _____it_____
3 the girl _____
5 the dogs _____

Down

2 the boys _____
3 the mother _____
4 the dog _____

	1 i	2 t	
	3		
4			
5			

38 unit 9 Pronouns

Review 3 — Review of Unit 7 to Unit 9

> He had / did not have a ticket.
> Did he have a ticket? Yes, he did./No, he didn't.

1 Write about the pictures.

She <u>had</u> a sandwich.

1 She _____ _____ _____ a cake.

2 _____ she _____ a cake? No, she didn't.

3 He _____ a lollipop.

4 He _____ _____ _____ a burger.

5 _____ he _____ a lollipop? Yes, he did.

Score ____ /5

> You must be quiet.
> You must not run.
> Must we read this book? Yes, you must.

2 Complete the school rules with *must* or *must not*.

You <u>must</u> be polite.

1 You _____ be late.

2 You _____ shout in class.

3 You _____ do your homework.

4 You _____ run in the school.

5 _____ we wear a uniform? Yes, you _____

Score ____ /5

Review 3

> She bought a dress.
> She did not buy a T-shirt.
> What did she buy? A dress.

3 Write about the pictures.

Go
He _went_ to school

1 He _____ _____ _____ to the beach.
2 Where _____ _____ _____? To school.

see
3 She _____ a duck.
4 She _____ _____ _____ a cow.
5 What _____ _____ _____? A duck.

Score ___ /5

> He is taller than Amy.
> He is the tallest.

4 Write sentences. Use the adjectives.

strong   Rory is _stronger_ than Joe.
young   Dan is _____

1 old   Rory is _____ than Dan.
2 strong Joe is _____
3 tall   Joe is _____
4 short   Dan is _____ than Joe.
5 thin   Rory is _____

Joe   Dan   Rory

Score ___ /5

40 Review 3

Review 3 — Review of Unit 1 to Unit 3

> Why is he working? Because he has a test.

5 Write questions and answers.

he / laugh <u>Why is he laughing?</u>   he / happy <u>Because he is happy.</u>
1 she / wear a coat _____?   Because it is a cold day.
2 Why are they eating?   they / hungry _____
3 you / read _____?   Because this book is good.
4 Why are they swimming?   it / hot day _____
5 he / sleep _____?   Because he is tired.

Phonics and spelling

5 Write and say.

1 y   sky
2
3   onayn _____
4
5 oy
6   joeny _____

7
8   oa
9
10

Score ___ /10

☺ 20–25   ☺ 26–30   ☺ 31–35

My score is _____.

Review 3   41

Review 3

Your Writing Page

1 Complete the story about the picture. Use the words in the box.

| jellyfish | my class | lemonade | Tuesday | aquarium |
| must not use | pizzas | must be quiet | a great time |

On _____ I went to the _____ with _____ . You _____ in the aquarium. You _____ your mobile phone. We saw fish, crabs and _____ . We didn't see a shark. We had _____ and _____ for lunch. We had _____ !

2 Write about the picture. Use the words in the box.

Wednesday	farm	with my friends
be careful on the farm	run on the farm
sheep	cows	horses	cat
burgers	orange juice	a good day

On <u>Wednesday I went</u> _____
_____
_____
_____
_____
_____

42 Review 3

Unit 10

I am going to swim.

He is going to play basketball.

1 Choose.

1 He — is / isn't — going to read a book.

2 She — is / isn't — going to read a book.

3 They — are / aren't — going to swim.

4 They — are / aren't — going to play football.

5 Is he / Is she — going to draw? No, he — is. / isn't

6 Is he / Is she — going to draw? Yes, she — is. / isn't.

2 Write questions. Match with the answers.

he / swim

1 <u>Is he going to swim?</u> <u>d</u>   a He's going to play tennis.

she / play tennis

2 _____? ____   b Yes, they are.

they / ride bicycles

3 _____? ____   c No, she isn't.

what / he / play

4 _____? ____   d Yes, he is.

Unit 10 Grammar 43

I'd like a sandwich.

Would you like a hot dog?
No, thank you.
How about a juice?
Yes, please.

1 Write in the correct order.

Would you like a sandwich?   No, thank you.
sandwich / like / a / Would / you

_____?   No, thank you.
a / How / pizza / about /

_____?   _____
you / What / like / would /   have / salad / going / am / I / a / to /

2 Follow the lines and complete the dialogues.

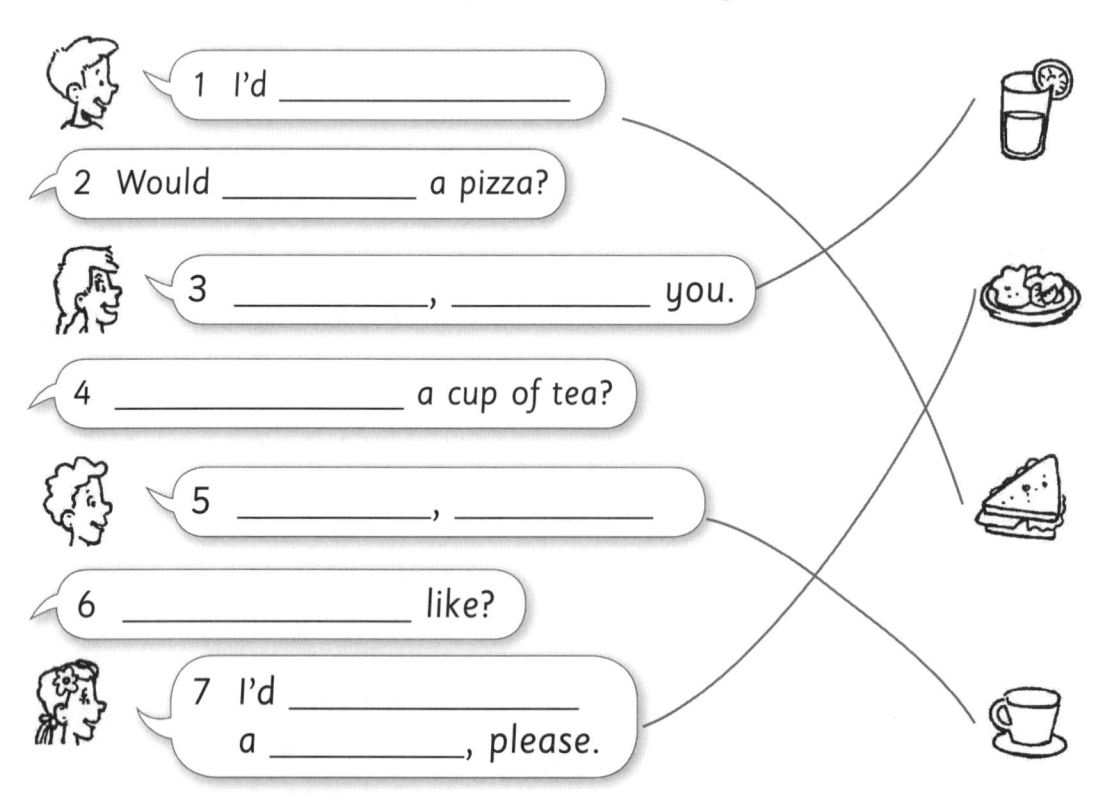

1 I'd _____

2 Would _____ a pizza?

3 _____, _____ you.

4 _____ a cup of tea?

5 _____, _____

6 _____ like?

7 I'd _____
   a _____, please.

44 Unit 10   Grammar in conversation

1 Write sentences and questions about the people in the picture.

1 go on the Mega ride

She <u>is going to go on the Mega ride.</u>

2 see a film <u>He is not going to see a film.</u>

3 have lunch _____

4 take a photo _____

5 take a photo <u>Is she going to take a photo?</u> No, she isn't.

6 buy a t-shirt _____? Yes, he is.

2 Complete the dialogue in the restaurant.

1 What _____ you _____?

2 I'd _____ a burger, _____

Use of English

3 Add punctuation.

1 Hello said the boy

2 Be careful said the teacher

3 What's the matter said the boy

4 There's a spider on your chair said the teacher

Unit 10 Speech marks for direct speech   45

Unit 11

There is some juice in the jug.
There is not any bread.
Are there any cakes? Yes, there are.
Is there any bread? No, there isn't.

1 Complete.

1 There _____ _____ cheese.
2 There _____ _____ sandwiches.
3 There _____ _____ _____ sweets.
4 _____ there any apples? Yes, there _____
5 _____ there any chicken? No, there isn't.
6 _____ there _____ grapes? Yes, there _____

2 Write.

1 <u>There are not any apples.</u>
2 _____
3 _____.
4 <u>Is there any cheese?</u> No, there isn't.
5 _____? No, there isn't.

46 Unit 11 Grammar

> What have you got? 
>
> I have got some eggs. I have not got any cheese.
>
> Has she got any cheese? No, she hasn't.

1 Write in the correct order. Match with the people.

a   b

got / I / some / have / sandwiches

1 _____ _____

not / have / got / I / cheese / any

2 _____ _____

any / got / you / have / fruit / ?

3 _____ _____? Yes, I have.

you / have / what / got / ?

4 _____?

some / got / chicken / have / I

_____ _____

2 Write about the people and their baskets.

✓ He / juice   1 <u>He has got some juice.</u>
  She / chicken   2 _____
✗ She / sweets   3 <u>She has not got any sweets</u>
  He / chocolate   4 _____
? He / fruit.   5 <u>Has he got any fruit?</u> No, he hasn't.
  She / water   6 _____? Yes, she has.

Unit 11 Grammar in conversation 47

1 Write about Zara's lunch.

1 sandwich <u>There is a sandwich.</u>

2 cake _____

3 grapes <u>Are there any grapes?</u>

   Yes, there are.

4 bread _____

   Yes, there is.

5 cheese _____

   No, there isn't.

In the Grammar Castle Café yesterday

2 Complete the conversation.

What _____ got?

<u>I've got some</u> bread.
_____ cheese.
_____ grapes.

Use of English

2 Write.

I like 🍦 🍎 🧁

1 <u>I like ice cream, apples and cakes.</u>

He has 🚲 📷 ✂️

2 _____

They saw 🐘 🦁 🐍 at the zoo

3 _____

Unit 11 Using commas with *and*

Unit 12

This book is mine.

Whose book is this?

It's hers.

1 Choose.

1 This book is his. / theirs.

2 Who / Whose car is that?

3 It's mine. / me.

4 These bikes are yours. / ours.

5 That house is hers. / theirs.

2 Write.

1 This is my pencil. It's _mine._

2 That is your car. It's _____

3 That is their house. It's _____

4 This is her cat. It's _____

5 This is our car. It's _____

6 This is his notebook. It's _____

Unit 12 Grammar 49

> When's your birthday?
>
> It's on the tenth of September.

1 Write the dates.

October 30 — 1 the thirtieth of October

April 3 — 4 _____

May 9 — 2 _____

February 1 — 5 _____

August 16 — 3 _____

Septmber 22 — 6 _____

2 Write questions and answers.

1 When is Tom's birthday?
   It's on the twentieth of March.

March — Tom 20

2 _____?
   _____

June — Amy 2

3 _____?
   _____

November — Angela 30

4 _____?
   _____

December — Ryan 17

50 unit 12 Grammar in conversation

Grammar Castle

1 Write questions and answers about the events.

- March — TV competition 6
- April — Spring Party 8
- June — Summer Fair 21
- October — Autumn Dance 21
- January — Winter Party 4

1 When is the TV competition?   It's on 6th March.
2 _____ ?   _____
3 _____ ?   _____
4 _____ ?   _____
5 _____ ?   _____

2 Complete with posessive pronouns.

1 I'm Tom. This book is _____ 
2 Jack is my friend. This book is _____ 
3 Lucy is my sister. This book is _____ 
4 Jim and Joe are my brothers. This book is _____

Use of English

3 Write the plural forms of the words.

1 lorry lorries
2 dress _____
3 key _____
4 lunch _____
5 boy _____
6 city _____
7 box _____
8 butterfly _____
9 baby _____

Unit 12 Plurals

Review 4 — Review of Unit 10 to Unit 12

> He is going to work.
> He is not going to swim.

1 Write in the correct order.

going / they / buy / to / lollipops / are <u>They are going to buy lollipops.</u>

1 cook / to / I / going / am / lunch / _____
2 the tree / not / he / going / climb / to / is _____
3 to / you / fall / going / are _____
4 travel / we / in a bus / going / not / are / to _____
5 a picture / she / to / is / going / draw _____

> Is he going to work? Yes, he is. / No, he isn't.
> What is he going to do? He's going to play basketball.

Score ____ /5

2 Complete the questions and answers.

<u>Are</u> you going <u>to</u> swim? Yes, I <u>am.</u>

1 Are you _____ to read a book? _____, I am.
2 _____ she going _____ fetch the water? No, _____ isn't.
3 _____ they _____ to win the prize? Yes, they _____
4 What _____ he going _____ cook? He's _____ to cook chicken.
5 _____ are they going _____ do? They're going _____ play computer games.

Score ____ /5

Review 4

> There is some water. / There is not any water.
> I've got some apples.

3 Complete the sentences.

There __are__ some grapes in the basket.

1 There _____ not any water in the jug.
2 There _____ not any apples in the basket.
3 There _____ some juice in the bottle.
4 She's got _____ apples.
5 She hasn't got _____ juice.

> Is there any water? Are there any cakes?
> Have you got any apples? Yes, I have.

Score ____ /5

4 Complete with is, are or any.

__Is__ there any water?   Yes, there _____

1 _____ there any cakes?   Yes, there _____
2 _____ there _____ bread?   No, there isn't.
3 _____ there _____ lollipops?   No, there aren't.
4 Have you got _____ pencils?   Yes, I have.
5 Has she got _____ chocolate?   No, she hasn't.

Score ____ /5

Review 4 53

Review 4

This bike is mine / yours / his / hers / ours / theirs.
When is your birthday? It's on the 15th of October.
Would you like a sandwich? Yes, please. / No, thank you. I'd like a juice.

5 **Write in the correct order.**

hat / yours / is / This /   This hat is yours.
birthday / on / 19th / is / My / May /   1 _____
a / like / pizza / you / Would /   2 _____?
books / theirs / Those / are /   3 _____
her / When / birthday / is /   4 _____?
mine / That / is / ice cream /   5 _____?

Phonics and spelling

6 **Write and say.**

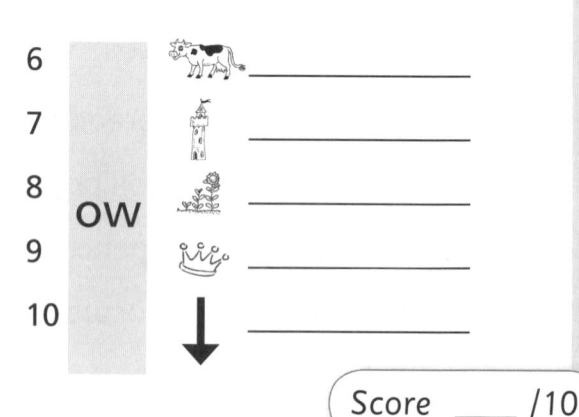

1 ur   burn
2   _____
3   _____
4 or   _____
5   _____

6   _____
7   _____
8 ow   _____
9   _____
10   _____

Score ____ /10

☺ 20–25   ☺ 26–30   ☺ 31–35

My score is _____.

54 Review 4

Review 4

Your Writing Page

1 Complete the story about the picture. Use the words in the box.

> juice   sandwiches   a party   cheese
> good   my friend's house   grapes

We are making the food for _____. There are some _____ and there is some _____. There are apples, oranges and _____. There is not any _____. There are not any sweets. We are going to have the party at _____. It's going to be a _____ party.

3 Write about the picture. Use the words in the box.

> picnic   pizzas   lemonade   cakes
> sandwiches   apples   ice cream   lollipops
> in the park   a good picnic

We are making the food for a _____.
_____
_____
_____
_____
_____
_____
_____
_____

Review 4   55

Macmillan Education
Between Towns Road, Oxford OX4 3PP
A division of Macmillan Publishers Limited
Companies and representatives throughout the world

ISBN 978-0-230-03206-4

Text © Nicholas Beare 2009
Design and illustration © Macmillan Publishers Limited 2009

First published 2009

All rights reserved; no part of this publication may be reproduced, stored in a retrieval system, transmitted in any form, or by any means, electronic, mechanical, photocopying, recording, or otherwise, without the prior written permission of the publishers.

Designed by Anthony Godber
Typeset by Wild Apple Design
Illustrated by Juliet Breese and Chantal Kees
Cover design by Oliver Design

The publishers would like to thank the following for their participation in the development of this course:
In Egypt – Inas Agiz, Salma Ahmed, Hekmat Aly, Suzi Balaban, Mohamed Eid, Bronwen El Kholy, Mostafa El Makhzangy, Hala Fouad, Jonathan French, Nashaat Nageeb Gendy, Hisham Howeedy, Saber Lamey, Heidi Omara, Maha Radwan, Amany Shawkey, Christine Abu Sitta, Ali Abdel Wahab

In Russia – Tatiana Antonova, Elena Belonozhkina, Galina Dragunova, Irina Filonenko, Marina Gaisina, Maria Goretaya, Oksana Guzhnovskaya, Irina Kalinina, Olga Kligerman, Galina Kornikova, Lidia Kosterina, Sergey Kozlov, Irina Larionova, Irina Lenchenko, Irina Lyubimova, Karine Makhmuryan, Maria Pankina, Anna Petrenkova, Elena Plisko, Natalia Vashchenko, Angelika Vladyko

Printed and bound in Malaysia

2012
10 9 8 7 6 5